FOUR-SUIT
TRANSFERS

Barbara Seagram & Andy Stark

MASTER POINT PRESS • TORONTO

PRACTICE YOUR BIDDING

Master Point Press
331 Douglas Avenue
Toronto, Ontario, Canada
M5M 1H2

(416) 781-0351   Internet: www.masterpointpress.com

National Library of Canada Cataloguing in Publication

Seagram, Barbara
          Four-suit Transfers / Barbara Seagram & Andy Stark.

(Practice your bidding)
ISBN 1-894154-86-X

1. Contract bridge--Bidding. I. Stark, Andy II. Title. III. Series: Seagram, Barbara. Practice Your Bidding.

GV1282.4.S4192 2004   795.41'52   C2004-902174-5

We acknowledge the financial support of the Government of Canada through the Book Publishing Industry Development Program (BPIDP) for our publishing activities.

Design and layout: Olena S. Sullivan/New Mediatrix
Editor: Ray Lee

Printed in Canada
1 2 3 4 5 6 7   10 09 08 07 06 05 04

TABLE OF CONTENTS

The
PRACTICE YOUR BIDDING
Series

Jacoby 2NT

Roman Keycard Blackwood

Splinter Bids

Jacoby Transfers

Four-Suit Transfers

Stayman Auctions

Practice Your Slam Bidding (CD-ROM)

Practice Your Notrump Bidding (CD-ROM)

section

HOW TO USE THIS BOOK

1

The purpose of this book is to help you and your partner practice Four-suit Transfers and better understand how they are used. The book has been designed so that it can be used either on your own or working with a partner. But while you will certainly get a lot out of it alone, it is especially good to use this book with your favorite partner to make sure that you are both on the same wavelength.

The first section of the book provides a refresher on Four-suit Transfers. It provides examples but no exercises. Don't worry, you will get plenty of chance to practice in the rest of the book. We have assumed in our example auctions that you are also playing Stayman, Gerber, and Roman Keycard Blackwood (all these are explained in detail in other books in this series). For more explanations, and as a source of other helpful conventions, you can also refer to *25 Bridge Conventions You Should Know*, by Barbara Seagram & Marc Smith, and *25 More Bridge Conventions You Should Know*, by Barbara Seagram & David Bird.

The last section of the book, 'Practice Hands', contains a set of forty pairs of North and South hands. You can cut them out or copy them and use them for a partner to practice bidding (don't try to do more than ten at one sitting — that's more than enough to think and talk about at one time). We have provided space beside each hand to write down your auction; we suggest that you do this so you can refer to it when you are looking at the answers. You can also do this solo if you like: look at each hand in turn and write down the bid you would make at each step of the auction. Getting to the right spot is not the only goal; bidding the hand in the best way is another goal, so even if you see both hands you will still need to work out the correct auction. When you have finished bidding the hands, look at the sample auctions and final contracts provided. There may be more than one way to bid the hand, so don't worry if you don't duplicate our sequence exactly. Focus in particular on your use of Four-suit Transfers, if it is appropriate, and the auction that follows, and make sure that you get that right.

There is an earlier section of the book, entitled 'Working Alone', which contains the same practice deals. In this section, we show you just one of the hands and ask you a series of questions about how to bid it as the auction develops. Working through these exercises will teach you a lot more about the convention, so even if you go through the practice deals with a partner, we suggest you go through the questions and try to answer them. This will help you to make sure that you understand the convention thoroughly.

The next chapters will provide you with plenty of opportunity to practice your transfer methods over 1NT opening bids. A few of the example hands and deals will test your knowledge of major-suit transfers, but for the most part this book concentrates on transfers to the minors. For a more comprehensive discussion of auctions involving transfer bids to the majors, please read the book *Jacoby Transfers* in this series.

A final warning: don't expect to be perfect. Some of these hands are hard. So if you are doing better at the end of the book than at the beginning, you are doing very well indeed.

HOW FOUR-SUIT TRANSFERS WORK

Why play Four-suit Transfers?

Four-suit Transfers are bids used directly after a 1NT opening. The first transfer system, called Jacoby Transfers, only catered to the majors. However, playing Four-suit Transfers the partner of the 1NT bidder can now transfer to *all four* suits. Think of this convention as 'Jacoby Transfers Extended'.

One purpose of extending transfer bids to the minors is to acquire all the advantages of having the strong hand, the 1NT bidder, play the hand, just as in Jacoby Transfers. However, Four-suit Transfers also allow the partnership to bid more effectively. How so? Well, in addition to other advantages that we'll see later, close games can be bid. Have you ever played in three of a minor only to discover 3NT was laydown? Yes, sometimes those 23- or 24-point games are reachable — as long as the partnership knows that six or seven tricks in either clubs or diamonds are there for the taking.

There's no guesswork, no 'shooting' or gambling; instead, you learn to evaluate and describe your hand at a slightly more advanced level, thus allowing you to bid better. Here's a sample hand:

♠ Q J 8 3		♠ 10 7
♡ K J 9		♡ 10 3
◇ A Q 10		◇ 8 7 6
♣ K 9 2		♣ A Q 10 8 5 4

Many pairs would bid these cards up to three clubs and most likely make it. But upon viewing the combination, wouldn't you say the ideal spot is 3NT? Six club tricks are assured. The ace of diamonds is the seventh and declarer has excellent prospects for two more tricks. If the opponents attack spades, for example, they will only be doing declarer a favor.

Now let's tweak the West hand a little bit; let's give West stronger spade and diamond holdings but weaker clubs:

♠ A 6 5 3   ♠ 10 7
♡ K J 9   ♡ 10 3
◇ A K J 4   ◇ 8 7 6
♣ 7 3   ♣ A Q 10 8 5 4

While 3NT might make with a friendly club position — that is, the king and jack of clubs are 'onside', able to be finessed — most of the time 3NT is going down. Another important consideration is that sometimes when 3NT is going down, it's going down a lot. So you would want to stop in three clubs with this combination of cards.

What is the main difference between the two hands? It has nothing to do with point count: it all depends on the club position. When the 1NT bidder has the king of clubs, six club tricks are ready for the taking. But when he holds a weak doubleton, only *one* club trick is assured.

Playing Four-suit Transfers allows the partnership to 'divine' their trick-taking potential in one of the minor suits. Knowing about good fits not only allows you to bid close games but it will tighten up your slam bidding too. Most of us tend to miss minor-suit slams because we are programmed to bid 3NT all the time and ignore minor-suit fits. Playing Four-suit transfers will help you find minor-suit slams too.

The next few pages will show you how to transfer to the minors. Once you learn how easy minor-suit transfer bids are, you will soon be bidding those close game contracts *and* staying out of the poor game contracts. In addition, your slam bidding will improve.

How do you transfer?

Similar to Jacoby Transfers, in Four-suit Transfers each of Responder's transfer bids are made *underneath* the suit he intends to show. Therefore,

1NT — 2◊	=	5+ hearts	
1NT — 2♡	=	5+ spades	
1NT — 2♠	=	6+ clubs	
1NT — 2NT	=	6+ diamonds (don't forget this one!)	

Notice that the transfers to the minors are made two levels below the suit you have, and notice also that you can no longer use 2NT as a natural game invitation over a 1NT opening. More on both these points later.

As you probably already know, when you transfer to hearts or spades you only require a minimum of five cards in your major. However, when you transfer to clubs or diamonds you will need at least six cards in that particular minor.

Why do you need a six-card minor? There are a couple of reasons. The most important is that by transferring to a minor you take partner to the three-level. If you are going to choose a minor suit contract over a 1NT contract (because you are weak), you need a little bit more security, and that can be realized with an extra trump. Since partner only promises two in any one suit when he opens 1NT, you will need six if you want to place the contract in 3♣ or 3◊.

Secondly, as you saw in the first example of this book, it is possible to reach good games with only 24 or even 23 HCP between the two hands. To make these kinds of precarious contracts a reasonable proposition, again we need some safety. The sixth card of a minor might only be a small spot-card, but it could be the contract-fulfilling trick. Obviously bidding game on a 4-3-3-3 hand opposite a 4-3-3-3 hand requires a full 26 HCP combined, but if one hand contains a six- or perhaps even a seven-card suit, then aggressive game contracts (those with fewer than 26 HCP) may be bid. As you read through this book you will see plenty of examples in which 3NT is the desired spot even when the combined assets total less than 26 HCP.

Another reason why you require six cards in a minor suit in order to transfer to that minor can be illustrated in the following example. Say your partner opens the bidding 1NT and you hold:

♠ 5 4   ♡ A 10 9   ◇ K 8 7   ♣ K J 10 7 6

What is your most descriptive bid? Let's say you could transfer to clubs. After doing so you would most certainly bid 3NT next, right? So the question remains, why would you ever want to show your clubs on this hand? Yes, it is barely possible that only a contract of five clubs is makable while 3NT is going down, but those hand types are rare. No, the correct call is an immediate 3NT. In fact, as soon as your partner opens the bidding 1NT you should breathe a sigh of relief, bid 3NT, and defy the opponents to beat the contract.

If, however, the hand is altered a little, so that the five of spades becomes the five of hearts, and the eight of diamonds becomes the eight of clubs, well that's a different story.

♠ 4   ♡ A 10 9 5   ◇ K 7   ♣ K J 10 8 7 6

Now 3NT is only a good contract if partner has two or three stoppers in spades. Plus, with such a lovely hand, isn't a contract of six clubs or six hearts worth investigating? (We'll talk about how to find that potential heart fit a little later.) Absolutely, and playing Four-suit Transfers allows you to investigate a slam without going past 3NT (which may be the last making contract). In effect, transfers allow you to have your cake and eat it too. But that sixth card in your minor is essential. With a sixth club or diamond card you are interested in both notrump and a minor-suit contract; without it, you are interested primarily in notrump.

What does opener do over the transfer?

So far you have looked at transferring to a minor from the point of view of the hand with length in the minor. What about opener? What should he do after a transfer bid has been made? The answer: *it all depends on his holding in that particular minor.*

With good support for responder's suit, at least K-x-x or A-x-x, opener should 'break the transfer'. That is, opener should not bid the suit that responder is showing — *instead, opener should bid the step in-between*. To illustrate, let's look at the two possible 'break the transfer' situations:

Partner	You
1NT	2♠[1]
2NT	

1. Showing six clubs.

Partner	You
1NT	2NT[1]
3♣	

1. Showing six diamonds.

In these auctions, partner is showing at least K-x-x- or A-x-x in your minor — clubs and diamonds respectively.

These transfer breaks don't say anything about whether the 1NT opener has a minimum or maximum strength hand. The governing principle for opener is to indicate how well his hand fits responder's minor suit. It's not about points, it's about the fit. So, with A-x-x or K-x-x, break the transfer and inform partner of the excellent fit.

What does opener do with any other holding, such as three small or a doubleton (however strong)? Simple. He just accepts the transfer and bids the suit his partner is showing.

Partner	You
1NT	2♠
3♣	

Partner	You
1NT	2NT
3♦	

This time, in each case partner is saying 'Whatever I have in your suit, it is worse than K-x-x.'

Weak hands

It's easy to understand the advantage of using transfer bids when you hold a weak hand. Why? Because you don't want your partner to go down one, two or three in a 1NT contract. Without transfers to the minors in their arsenal, many players have to go through some sort of Stayman sequence. Aside from the subtle drawbacks of this method (like allowing the opponents more room to get into the bidding), sequences like the following give away information, and get the contract played from the wrong (weak) side:

Partner	You
1NT	2♣
2♡	3♣[1]
pass	

1. Drop-dead bid in clubs.

Playing Four-suit Transfers, with hands such as these:

a) ♠ J ♡ 10 3 ◇ 4 3 2 ♣ J 10 8 6 5 4 3

b) ♠ 10 2 ♡ 8 7 6 ◇ 6 5 ♣ K 10 7 6 5 3

the auction would proceed:

Partner	You
1NT	2♠
3♣	pass

Without even seeing opener's hand, surely 3♣ is the most comfortable contract. Granted, 1NT could be laydown if partner holds the right cards, but whatever those 'right cards' are, 3♣ will be making too. Also, in both cases, if partner were to surprise you with a transfer break, you would still sign off in 3♣:

Partner	You
1NT	2♠
2NT	3♣

Try as you might, you still can't see how partner is going to muster nine tricks in a notrump contract, even if your suit is worth six tricks. Put hand (b) opposite a typical hand for partner:

♠ A J 2	♠ 10 2
♡ Q J 9	♡ 8 7 6
◇ K 8 7 3	◇ 6 5
♣ A 9 8	♣ K 10 7 6 5 3

This is one of those hands where notrump could go down a lot, but a contract of 3♣ rates to do very well. Forget about playing 3NT, even if the clubs do turn out to be worth six tricks. Even 24-point games are enough of a stretch; 18-point games are for basketball players.

Invitational hands

Invitational hands are fun to bid because they are analogous to a common everyday real-life occurrence. Say you are about to enter a doorway at the same time as someone else. You hold the door open for this person and say, "After you," and that person in turn stops, holds the door open for you, and says, *"No, after you."*

When you hold a hand in which you plan to invite partner to game, because you have a six-card minor and say, 7-9 HCP, you begin by making your normal transfer bid. But partner has the option of inviting you to game first, which he does by breaking the transfer. Now that you are enlightened with the knowledge of partner's holding in your minor suit, you can bid on to game if you want.

Suppose partner opens 1NT and you hold one of the following hands:

a) ♠ Q 2   ♡ 6 4 3   ◇ 9 8   ♣ A Q 9 4 3 2
b) ♠ 9 7 4   ♡ -   ◇ 8 7 5 4   ♣ A Q 10 9 5 4
c) ♠ 4   ♡ 4 3   ◇ K Q J 8 7 4 3   ♣ J 6 5

With (a) and (b) you plan to transfer to clubs, then listen (or watch) intently for partner's rebid. If he rebids 2NT, showing ♣K-x-x or better, you will bid 3NT because you like your chances in that contract. Your club suit rates to be worth six tricks.

On hand (c) you plan to transfer to diamonds. Again, if partner breaks the transfer with 3♣, you will place the contract in 3NT. This time your hand is worth seven tricks.

Typically, invitational hands contain 7-9 HCP but sometimes if you want to be aggressive you can upgrade a 6-point hand — provided you have the ace and queen of your six-card minor and partner indicates the king with his rebid. You know that partner has at least twelve other high-card points with which to garner three more tricks.

What happens to the 'standard' auction 1NT-2NT?

One of the auctions you sacrifice when you adopt Four-suit Transfers is this common start: you open the bidding 1NT and partner responds 2NT. Traditionally this bid promised 8-9 HCP and a fairly balanced hand, and invited you to bid 3NT with a maximum.

But you can no longer bid this way. If partner bids 2NT over your 1NT opening you must remember that now he is showing diamonds. Oh sure, he *may* actually have 8 or 9 HCP, but the thing to remember is that he *certainly* has a hand with long diamonds; in fact, he could be either very weak or very strong! So don't pass, and for heaven's sake, don't bid 3NT: simply bid 3◊, or break the transfer with 3♣ (if you have good enough diamond support).

All right then, you no doubt are wondering what you should do with a balanced 8-9 HCP opposite a 1NT opening bid. The answer may surprise you: start with 2♣, Stayman. Then after you hear partner's 2◊ or 2♡ or 2♠, rebid 2NT. This sequence does not promise a four-card major, it merely promises 8-9 points and is invitational to 3NT. To review,

Partner	You
1NT	2NT

This shows diamonds.

Partner	You
1NT	2♣
any	2NT

This promises 8-9 HCP, balanced.

Strong one-suited hands

Before we explain how to bid strong hands that contain a six-card minor, first ask yourself if the nature of your hand is a single-suiter. If so, then the best methods are old-fashioned ones, which we'll review first.

Say you hold:

♠ A 3   ♡ 4 3   ◊ A Q J 9 8 4   ♣ K 9 6

Instead of transferring to diamonds, you should simply bid diamonds yourself at the three-level. Now that you are playing

Four-suit Transfers, this bid promises 6+ diamonds and a game-forcing, single-suited hand. Partner will look at his hand and determine how well his hand is suited for a diamond slam and then let you know his opinion with his rebid. For example, after 1NT-3◇, if partner bids a new suit he is indicating a good hand for a diamond slam. How does partner know if his hand is good for diamonds? By adding up the positive features of his hand. Positive features include:

- A good fit for diamonds — any three or more diamonds

- maximum strength hand, 16+ to 17 HCP

- controls — aces and kings, not queens and jacks

So a new suit by partner after your 3◇ bid will express a positive opinion about a diamond slam. Also, partner's bid will promise first-round control in that particular suit. Here's a deal to illustrate:

Partner	You
♠ Q 8 7 2	♠ A 3
♡ A K 6 5	♡ 4 3
◇ K 10 5	◇ A Q J 9 8 4
♣ A 8	♣ K 9 6
1NT	3◇
3♡	3♠
4NT	5♠
6◇	pass

Both 3♡ and 3♠ are control-showing cuebids. Partner has enough information to ask for keycards via 4NT, and 5♠ shows two keycards plus the trump queen. The final contract of 6◇ is laydown unless the opponents can ruff something at Trick 1. Nice bidding. (For further explanation of Roman Keycard Blackwood and control-showing cuebids, you are referred to other titles in this series.)

What does partner do when he does not like his hand for your minor? He bids 3NT. After you have shown slam interest with a jump to either 3♣ or 3◇, 3NT is a 'slowdown' bid by partner. Typically he has negative features such as:

- a poor fit for your minor (usually a weak doubleton)

- a minimum strength hand — 15 HCP

- poor controls — few aces and kings, lots of queens and jacks

For example, say you have the same hand as above, but this time partner holds:

Partner	You
♠ Q 8 7	♠ A 3
♡ K Q J 6	♡ 4 3
◇ 10 7	◇ A Q J 9 8 4
♣ A Q J 8	♣ K 9 6

Partner opens 1NT and you bid 3◇. With a doubleton diamond, 15 HCP and only one ace and one king, partner will rebid 3NT and there you will play. Slam is at best on a finesse and a favorable trump break, so 3NT is definitely the right spot. More nice bidding!

Transferring with a strong hand

Now it gets really interesting. With a game-forcing hand containing six cards in a minor and at least four in a major, show your minor first, then the major.

♠ A Q J 8   ♡ 4   ◇ A J 10 8 7 5   ♣ Q 9

If partner opens 1NT, begin with a transfer to diamonds, then rebid spades — natural and game-forcing. Partner will now describe his hand with one of five possible calls. He may raise either diamonds (with three) or spades (with four) to show his support there. Or he will bid 3NT to deny support for either of your suits and discourage you from bidding a slam. Finally he may cuebid clubs or hearts. The cuebid is the strongest bid he can make because it implies interest in one of your suits and is forward-going. Specifically it promises first-round control (the ace) in the suit bid.

The following hands reflect some of partner's choices. What is partner's most descriptive bid in each case after you have shown six-plus diamonds and four spades?

Partner	You
1NT	2NT
3♢	3♠
?	

a) ♠ K 3 2   ♡ K Q J 5   ♢ Q 9   ♣ K J 10 8
b) ♠ K 4 3 2   ♡ J 8 5 4   ♢ K 9   ♣ A K J

With (a) partner should bid 3NT. The negative features include the doubleton diamond, the 15 HCP's, and the lack of controls — he has no aces. With (c) the best bid is 4♠, promising four-card support. Now you can both continue to describe your hands and explore a spade slam.

To sum up this segment on strong hands, a little 'un-learning' is required. You have been taught to use 2♣ Stayman whenever you hold a four-card major. However, playing Four-suit Transfers your priority on strong hands is to show a six-card minor first and then to show your major-suit holding second. By bidding in this order (length before strength), partner will know at least ten of your cards. The corollary is that whenever you hold a four-card major and only a five-card minor, you will in fact begin with Stayman then rebid your minor suit, for example:

Partner	You
1NT	2♣
2♡	3♣

Partner will know your distribution accurately. Here, you have four spades, five clubs, and a game-going hand. This is a big change from when you just play Jacoby Transfers, where this auction shows six slubs, a weak hand, and not necessarily a four-card major at all!

Strong hands with both minors

For every rule there is an exception (and this rule is no exception). Confused? You should be. What we mean is, there is an exception to the rule of transferring only when you hold a six-card minor. You may, with 5-5 in the minors and a game-forcing hand, choose to transfer to diamonds and then show your clubs.

Partner	You
♠ K 8 3 2	♠ A
♡ A Q 10	♡ 4 3
◇ A 9	◇ K Q J 8 3
♣ Q 10 6 4	♣ A J 9 7 5
1NT	2NT
3◇	4♣
4♡	4♠
4NT	5♡
6♣	

After partner's 1NT opening you should plan to transfer to diamonds first, then show your clubs. Your 4♣ bid is natural and forcing. (Remember, partner's 3◇ bid denied A-x-x of diamonds, so by bidding on anyway you indicate slam interest.) Now partner is able to show his enthusiasm for clubs with a control-showing cuebid, 4♡. You return the favor with 4♠ and partner asks you for keycards. Your 5♡ shows two keycards and denies the queen of clubs. How do you know clubs is the trump suit? First, partner denied good diamond support with 3◇ (he failed to break the transfer), and then he implied club support with 4♡ — clubs is the trump suit.

WORKING ALONE (QUESTIONS)

Deal 1

♠ K 6
♡ K 5
◇ 8 5
♣ 10876432

1. Partner opens 1NT and you hold two kings and a seven-card suit. Will you drive the bidding to a game contract?
2. You bid 2♠ and partner breaks the transfer by bidding 2NT to show Kxx of clubs or better. Do you bid game now?

Deal 2

♠ —
♡ K Q 9 4
◇ 8 3
♣ AQ87643

1. Partner opens the bidding with 1NT; do you use Stayman or start with a transfer?
2. If you transfer to clubs, partner accepts the transfer by bidding 3♣. What do you bid now?
3. Say partner breaks the transfer with a rebid of 2NT; what do you bid? What do you think the final contract will be?

Deal 3

♠ 10 7 6
♡ 8 3
◇ K Q J 9 7 4
♣ 7 2

1. Partner opens 1NT and you transfer to diamonds by bidding 2NT. Partner breaks the transfer and bids 3♣. What do you bid and why?
2. If partner simply bids 3◇ over your 2NT bid, what do you do and why?

Deal 4

♠ Q J 8 4
♡ Q J
♢ Q J
♣ Q J 9 6 5

1. Partner opens 1NT; what are the only two contracts you are thinking of?
2. Do you begin by using Stayman or do you transfer to clubs?
3. If you bid 2♣, Stayman, partner responds 2♢; what do you bid next?

Deal 5

♠ 7 4
♡ 9
♢ K Q 10 8 3
♣ A 9 7 5 3

1. It would be nice to have a system over a 1NT opening whereby with one bid you can show 5/5 in the minors and a game-forcing hand. But you can still show this hand using Four-suit Transfers. What is your plan?
2. Say you transfer to diamonds; what is your next bid over either 3♣ or 3♢ by partner, and why?
3. Although 3NT might be the best contract, why is it better to give up on that contract and show your two-suited hand?

Deal 6

♠ A 8
♡ 7
♢ A J 9 8 4
♣ K Q 10 7 2

1. Partner opens 1NT and you immediately think of driving towards slam; how do you begin?
2. After transferring to diamonds and then bidding clubs, what will your next bid be?
3. If partner breaks the transfer to show Kxx of diamonds or better, what will your rebid be?

Deal 7

♠ K 10 9 7 3
♡ A 3
♢ 4
♣ A J 7 6 5

1. Partner opens 1NT and you transfer to spades. Partner dutifully bids 2♠ and you bid... what?
2. After you rebid 3♣, which is natural and game-forcing, partner bids 3♢; what is the meaning of this call? What is your next bid?

Deal 8

♠ A 5
♡ K 6
♢ A 8 4
♣ Q J 10 9 8 4

1. Partner opens 1NT and you decide to bid 2♠ to transfer to clubs.   What is your plan after partner's rebid of a) 2NT; b) 3♣?
2. Say you don't transfer to clubs, but instead you jump to 3♣ immediately over partner's 1NT opening?   What is the meaning of your bid?
3. If partner bids 3♡ over your jump to 3♣, what contract do you envision?   If partner instead bids 3NT over your bid of 3♣, what will you bid next?

Deal 9

♠ 7
♡ K 5 4
♢ K Q 9 7 6 4
♣ A 8 7

1. Partner opens 1NT; what is your plan on this hand?
2. If you jump to 3♢ and partner bids 3NT, what will you do next?
3. If, after your 3♢ bid, partner bids three of a major, what will you do next?

Deal 10

♠ A 3 2
♡ A 5 2
♢ A 4 3
♣ K 6 4 3

1. You open 1NT and partner transfers to clubs by bidding 2♠.   What do you rebid with your minimum 15 HCP?
2. If partner bids 3♣ next, do you bid again?

Deal 11

♠ A 8 6
♡ K 9 7
♢ Q J 5
♣ A K 9 8

1. You open 1NT and partner transfers to clubs. You break the transfer to show your delight with a club contract.   Partner bids 3♣, showing a weak hand and a long club suit; do you bid again?

Deal 12

♠ K Q 6 3
♡ 8 3
◇ A J 9 7 6 4
♣ 7

1. Partner opens 1NT; what is your plan?
2. If you transfer to diamonds, partner bids 3◇; what do you bid next?
3. If partner breaks the transfer, what is your call?

Deal 13

♠ Q 7
♡ Q 9 8
◇ K 4
♣ J 9 6 5 4 3

1. Partner opens 1NT; what is your plan?
2. If you transfer to clubs and partner rebids 3♣, do you bid again?

Deal 14

♠ Q 10 7 6 4
♡ K J 8 7 2
◇ 3
♣ A 2

1. Partner opens 1NT; which major do you transfer to first?
2. Say you transfer to spades, then bid hearts, are you promising 5-4 in the majors or 5-5?
3. If you transfer to spades and then bid 4♡, what does that show?

Deal 15

♠ Q 8 6 5 3
♡ 4
◇ A 9 8 4 3
♣ 10 7

1. You transfer to spades after partner's 1NT bid. What do you do after partner rebids 2♠?
2. What if partner super-accepts with 3♠?

Deal 16

♠ K 9
♡ 8
◇ A 8 4 3
♣ K J 10 9 6 2

1. Partner opens 1NT. Do you transfer to clubs or jump to 3♣ immediately?
2. Say the auction goes: 1NT-2♠, 3♣-3◇, 3NT-? Do you pass partner's bid of 3NT or do you bid 4♣?

Deal 17

♠ 5 3 2
♡ 7 3
◇ 8 2
♣ A K Q 4 3 2

1. Partner opens the bidding with 1NT. Do you transfer to clubs or not?
2. If you decide not to transfer, what is your call?

Deal 18

♠ 6
♡ K 8 5 4 2
◇ 9
♣ K Q 9 5 4 3

1. This is tricky hand to describe after a 1NT bid by partner. You will start with a transfer bid, but which one? Will you transfer to hearts or clubs?
2. Say you transfer to clubs; what is your plan from there?

Deal 19

♠ 9 8
♡ 6
◇ Q 7 6 2
♣ K J 8 6 5 3

1. Partner opens 1NT and you transfer to clubs with a bid of 2♠. Partner breaks the transfer and bids 2NT. What do you know about his hand?
2. What do you bid now?

Deal 20

♠ 10 2
♡ 9 4
◇ K 10 9 7 5 4 3
♣ Q 8

1. Partner opens 1NT and you bid 2NT. What is your plan over a 3◇ response?
2. What will you do if partner finds a 3♣ response?

Deal 21

♠ K 7 5 4
♡ K J 9 2
◇ A K
♣ K 10 8

1. You open 1NT and partner transfers you to clubs. What do you bid?
2. You decide your hand is worth a textbook 2NT rebid. What is the key feature of your hand that make you happy to break the transfer?
3. After your 2NT bid, partner bids 3♡. You're such a good partner, you have support for everything partner bids. So now what?

Deal 22

♠ Q J 3 2
♡ Q 9 8 3
◇ A K
♣ Q J 4

1. You open 1NT and partner transfers you to clubs; what do you call?
2. What are features of your hand might cause you to bid a quiet 3♣?

Deal 23

♠ A 4
♡ A 8 7
◇ A Q 9
♣ Q J 7 5 2

1. Once again, you open 1NT and partner transfers you to clubs. There are two features of your hand that get you excited about clubs, but there is also one negative feature. So, which will it be — 3♣ or 2NT?
2. What would you have done if partner transferred you to diamonds?

Deal 24

♠ A Q 10 8 6 5
♡ 8
◇ A K 3
♣ Q 7 3

1. Partner opens 1NT. Do you transfer?
2. Say you jump the bidding to three spades, showing a game-forcing hand with six or more spades. What will you bid over partner's four potential rebids of 3NT, 4♣, 4♡ and 4♠?
3. Why are you not concerned that partner will bid 4◇ over your 3♠?

Deal 25

♠ 64
♡ 8
◇ 4
♣ J108765432

1. Wow, a nine-card suit opposite partner's 1NT opening! And partner promises two more clubs, making it at least an eleven-card fit. You know you want to play in a club contract but at what level?
2. Your options are: pass, 2♠ (transfer to clubs), and an immediate 3♣ or 5♣ — which do you prefer and why?

Deal 26

♠ A 10 7 3
♡ A 10 9 7
◇ A 10
♣ A 10 8

1. Aces and spaces? Not exactly -- those tens and nines are gold. What are your rebids after you open 1NT and partner bids one of the following:
   a) 2♣;
   b) 2◇;
   c) 2♡;
   d) 2♠;
   e) 2NT?

Deal 27

♠ A Q 10
♡ K 10 9
◇ A K 10 9 8
♣ 9 8

1. You open 1NT and partner transfers you to clubs; what is your call?
2. Say you bid 3♣ and partner bids 3♡; what do you bid now?

Deal 28

♠ 7
♡ J 9 7 5 4
◇ 6
♣ J 10 9 8 4 3

1. Partner opens 1NT and once again you are faced with a choice of transfers. Which suit do you transfer to and why?
2. Say you transfer to hearts; what do you do if partner super-accepts with 3♡?

Deal 29

♠ A J 4
♡ 9 8 6
◇ K 10 8 3
♣ J 7 2

1. Partner opens 1NT. What is your call?

Deal 30

♠ 8 6 4 3
♡ 9
♢ A K Q J 7 6
♣ A 3

1. Another tricky one, as you have lots of options here if partner opens 1NT. You could bid an immediate 3♢ or you could transfer. You might even begin with Stayman, although that is not recommended with a six-card minor. Well, any ideas how to respond to partner's 1NT opening?
2. Say you transfer to diamonds; what are you 100% sure partner is going to bid?
3. After partner bids the expected 3♢, what is your next bid?

Deal 31

♠ A 6 3
♡ K Q J 9 6
♢ K 10 3
♣ K 3

1. You open 1NT and partner transfers you to diamonds with 2NT. What is your bid?
2. If partner transferred you to clubs instead, what would you bid?
3. And just for good measure, what would be your rebid if partner transferred you to spades?

Deal 32

♠ 9 7
♡ 6 4 3
♢ A J 10 9 7 5
♣ Q 5

1. Partner opens 1NT. You hold a classic invitational hand . . . or do you? Should you transfer to diamonds or jump to 3NT?
2. Say you transfer; what will be your plan over partner's rebid of either 3♣ or 3♢?

Deal 33

♠ A 7
♡ K 10 8 7 6
♢ 2
♣ A 9 7 6 4

1. Partner opens 1NT and you transfer to hearts; what do you call after partner bids 2♡?
2. Say you bid 3♣ next; what are the messages you are sending with this sequence?
3. Assume partner bids 3♢ or 3♡ over 3♣, what will be your third call, something you probably envisioned from the beginning?

Deal 34

♠ K 5
♡ J 10 4
◇ J 9
♣ A 10 9 8 4 3

1. Partner opens 1NT. What is your call?
2. Why should you not transfer to clubs with this hand?

Deal 35

♠ K Q 8 7 6 5
♡ 10 8 3
◇ 7 3
♣ Q 4

1. Partner opens 1NT and again you transfer to spades. Partner rebids two spades, accepting your transfer; what is your next call?
2. If partner opened one club and you responded one spade, what would you do over partner's rebid of a) 2♣? b) 1NT?

Deal 36

♠ K 3
♡ K 5
◇ K Q J 10 8 6 4
♣ K 2

1. You are such a good cardholder! Partner opens 1NT. Do you transfer to diamonds?
2. Say you decide to use Gerber. You need to prepare each of your subsequent bids over partner's responses; what will you call if partner shows:
   a) 1 ace;
   b) 2 aces;
   c) 3 aces;
   d) 4 aces?

Deal 37

♠ 7
♡ A 10 9 7 3
◇ 9 7 6
♣ K J 4 3

1. Partner opens 1NT and you bid 2◇, transfer to hearts. Partner bids 2♡; what next?
2. What is wrong with a rebid of 3♣?
3. Say the auction proceeds: 1NT-2◇, 2♡-2NT, 3♡. What is your next call — 4♡ or pass?

Deal 38

♠ K 10 9 4 3
♡ 3
♢ Q J 7 6
♣ A 8 6

1. Partner opens 1NT and you bid 2♡, a transfer to spades. Partner bids 2♠ and you bid 3♢. Why is this a better bid than simply jumping to 3NT?
2. Say after you bid 3♢, partner returns to 3♠; what is the message of 3♠?
3. What will you bid next after partner bids 3♠ over your 3♢? And why?

Deal 39

♠ 10 8
♡ J 3 2
♢ 5 4
♣ A Q 10 8 7 4

1. Partner opens the bidding 1NT and you transfer to clubs. What is your plan from there?
2. If partner breaks the transfer, do you confidently bid 3NT or are you concerned about your porous holdings in the other three suits?
3. Why should you bid 3NT with confidence?

Deal 40

♠ K J 8 3
♡ Q 10 9 4
♢ A K
♣ K J 9

1. You open the bidding 1NT. What will you rebid over the following possible bids by partner: a) 2♣; b) 2♢; c) 2♡; d) 2♠; e) 2NT; f) 3♣; g) 3♢; h) 3♡; j) 3♠; k) 3NT?

WORKING ALONE (answers)

Deal 1

1. No, show your clubs and sign off. Your clubs are too weak. If your six points in the majors were concentrated in your club suit you might consider bidding a pushy game.

2. If you knew for sure that partner had A-K-x or A-K-x-x of clubs you might push to the game, but there is no way of ever knowing; take the sure plus and sign off in three clubs.

Deal 2

1. Transfer to clubs by bidding 2♠; keep Stayman for 5-4 hands.

2. Bid 3♡. This sequence promises six or more clubs and four hearts.

3. Bid 3♡ still — maybe you still have a heart fit. After partner's enthusiasm for clubs you are very close to a slam — if he can make a control-showing cuebid in diamonds, you're there.

Deal 3

1. Bid 3NT. Partner is promising at least A-x-x of diamonds for his bid of 3♣. Now your six points and six diamonds are good for six tricks. With luck, partner's remaining 11-13 HCP will produce the other three tricks he needs to make 3NT.

2. Pass 3♢. If partner does not have a good hand for diamonds then we are high enough. If partner holds three small diamonds, or even worse, a small doubleton, the opponents may be able to keep him from ever reaching the dummy in notrump. Yes, those diamonds might only be worth one trick.

Deal 4

1. The only two contracts you are considering on this hand are 3NT and 4♠.

2. Start with a bid of 2♣, Stayman. First check to see if there is a 4-4 fit in spades.

3. You should bid 3NT now. Although a bid of 3♣ would be forcing and descriptive, there really is no point when you know the best contract is 3NT. All your queen-jack combinations ('quacks') mean the hand will be best played in notrump.

Deal 5

1. There is no one quick bid to show a game-forcing hand with 5-5 in the minors, unless of course you have some special agreement with your partner. Here you should plan to transfer to diamonds and then bid clubs.

2. You should bid 4♣. As responder with an excellent two-suiter, you owe it to partner to describe your hand and let partner in on the decision-making.

3. By showing both minors on this hand you can get to good slams when partner has the right cards. The only drawback is that you bypass 3NT when that might be the best contract. Still, picture partner with:

     ♠ A K 6 3   ♡ 5 4 2   ◇ A 7 5 2   ♣ K Q 4

   and you can see that six diamonds is a great spot while 3NT is in danger of going down.

Deal 6

1. Once again you plan to show your diamonds and your clubs, and then later in the bidding, if necessary, show your spade control so that partner will know that suit is controlled.

2. Bid 4♠ after showing both of your minors.

3. If partner shows enthusiasm for diamonds by bidding 3♣ over your 2NT bid, you should simply bid 4NT, RKB for diamonds. If you discover partner has the diamond king and queen, and the club and heart aces, along with either major-suit king, you have a grand slam.

Deal 7

1. Bid 3♣ (natural and forcing to game) over partner's 2♠ call.

2. Partner's 3◇, after your 3♣ call, is a control-showing cuebid agreeing clubs as the trump suit. You should cuebid 3♡. You can imagine a lot of hands partner might hold that make 6♣ an excellent contract. The key is to show your controls.

Deal 8

1. Trick question! Remember with a single-suiter in clubs or diamonds, start by bidding that suit at the three-level. Don't transfer or else you will have a serious rebid problem.

2. By bidding 3♣ immediately you show a six-card or longer suit and a game-forcing or slam-try hand.

3. If partner can bid 3♡ over your 3♣ call, he is saying, 'I have this suit controlled (the ace) and a good fitting hand for your clubs.' Typically partner has an honor in clubs and a maximum 1NT opening with good controls. Slam is definitely a possibility, and you should cuebid 3♠ next. If, however, partner can only muster a bid of 3NT over 3♣, then pass; he probably has weak clubs and a minimum notrump with 'quacks'.

Deal 9

1. Once again, show your single-suited hand by jumping to the three-level; you should bid 3◇.

2. Pass. By jumping to 3◇ you enlist partner's co-operation. If partner bids 3NT he is saying he does not like his hand for a diamond contract. He might hold:

    ♠ K Q J 5   ♡ A 6 3   ◇ J 2   ♣ K Q 4 3

    Note that partner is close to cuebidding 3♡ here, but his ◇J-x of diamonds prevent him getting too excited about slam.

3. If partner makes a bid in a new suit, such as 3♠, bid 4♣ to show your first-round control there. For his 3♠ call, he might hold something like:

    ♠ A 6 5 2   ♡ Q 3   ◇ A J 2   ♣ K Q 4 3

    Now you are off to the races, and will not stop short of slam in diamonds.

Deal 10

1. Break the transfer! Partner did not ask whether you were minimum or maximum, just about your club holding. In fact, you hold excellent support in king-fourth of clubs. Bid 2NT.

2. No, you pass. As quickly as you super-accepted clubs, you pass his sign-off. You must respect partner's opinion and pass. The reason? Partner might hold:

♠ 6   ♡ 7 4 3   ◇ 6 5 2   ♣ 10 9 8 7 5 2

Deal 11

1. No, you pass. Yes a 17 -point maximum with A-K-x-x of clubs is wonderful, but partner heard your positive attitude towards a club contract, so let him make the final decision. Partner probably has something like:

♠ 3 2   ♡ 5 4   ◇ 6 4 2   ♣ J 7 6 4 3 2

Deal 12

1. You plan to show diamonds and spades. With a six-card minor and a forcing hand, show your minor suit first then bid your four-card major, a bid which will be natural and forcing. Start with 2NT, a transfer to diamonds.

2. 3♠ — this shows four spades and six-plus diamonds.

3. If partner were to break the diamond transfer, promising at least K-x-x of diamonds, you will know about a good nine-card fit. Although it looks tempting to bid Blackwood, you would be embarrassed by a 5♡ call, showing only two keycards. Therefore, even if partner breaks the transfer, simply bid 3♠ to show your four-card suit and game-forcing hand. Your best strategy with this hand is to keep describing.

Deal 13

1. Your plan is to invite partner to bid a game, but how? Transfer to clubs or Stayman and 2NT? With 7 of your 8 HCP *outside* of the club suit, we recommend going through Stayman. Start with 2♣ and no matter what partner replies (2◇, 2♡, 2♠), rebid 2NT. This sequence is an invitation to 3NT.

2. Who knows? This is partly why we recommend not bidding the hand this way! Say you transfer and partner bids 3♣; you really don't know what to do next. You might play there or you might close your eyes and accept your own invitation by bidding 3NT. Alternatively, say partner bids 2NT, a club super-accept. He could be making this bid on K-x-x of clubs and on a bad day you will still have three losers in the suit. Therefore the best approach is simply to invite partner to game based on your overall strength and let him decide.

Deal 14

1. This one is easy. You approach this hand the same way you would approach responding to an opening of one club or one diamond: by bidding spades first. So, transfer to spades first.

2. You are promising 5-5 in the majors and a hand with some slam interest if you transfer to spades and then rebid 3♡. With 5-4 in the majors you would begin with 2♣ Stayman (see the companion books *Stayman Auctions* and *Jacoby Transfers*.).

3. When you transfer to spades and rebid 4♡, you are simply asking partner to pick between 4♡ and 4♠. Your hand is likely not strong enough for slam.

Deal 15

1. This one is not easy. If partner merely bids 2♠ you should pass. You can't bid 3◇ as that shows a game-forcing hand and you don't have either the right strength or the right distribution to invite 3NT by bidding 2NT. Partscore is high enough.

2. However, over a super-accept bid of 3♠ by partner you should go for the game bonus and bid 4♠. The decision is made easier knowing partner has four spades and a maximum-strength hand. If he has a fitting card or two in the diamond suit, game will be practically laydown. The key with this hand is knowing about a good trump fit.

Deal 16

1. What a lovely problem! Actually, playing Four-suit Transfers you can have your cake and eat it too. Plan it this way:

transfer to clubs and then bid diamonds. This shows six clubs and four diamonds — it is the same strategy you would employ to show a six-card minor and a four-card major.

2. You should pass. Partner knows of your shape and strength, but he is suggesting 3NT as good final contract. You should respect his opinion knowing you have painted a good picture of your hand. Partner will have a lot of wasted values in the majors.

Deal 17

1. There is little point in transferring here: partner cannot possibly super-accept, and what are you going to do over his 3♣ rebid? Are you really interested in playing in clubs ?

2. You should simply bid 3NT — definitely not 3♣. You cannot have a better hand with 9 HCP: even if partner holds a worthless doubleton club, your hand rates to take six tricks. Is the notrump game going to be better than five clubs? Most of the time, yes; as the old bridge adage goes, it's easier to take nine tricks than eleven.

Deal 18

1. As Grant Baze wrote many years ago, '6-5, come alive'. Transfer to clubs first.

2. Transfer to clubs and then bid hearts twice giving partner a choice between four hearts or five clubs. You expect the auction to go something like this: 1NT-2♠, 3♣-3♡, 3NT-4♡. At this point partner knows you have six clubs and five hearts because you transferred first to clubs. With longer or equal hearts you would have transferred to hearts first.

Deal 19

1. Two features of partner's hand are: he has balanced distribution and he holds thirteen cards. Just kidding. Specifically, he holds 15-17 HCP, a balanced hand, the ace of clubs and at least three clubs in total. You know he has the ace of clubs because he broke the transfer and you are looking at the king.

2. You should bid 3NT. The value of your hand increases knowing about the nine-card club fit.

Deal 20

1. You will pass partner's bid of 3◇. This is a hand tailor-made for Four-suit Transfers. Why? Because you learn partner does not hold ◇A-x-x; therefore you know your dummy will not provide as many tricks as you would like in notrump.

2. However, if partner breaks the transfer, bid 3NT. If partner has at least ◇A-x-x, he can enter your hand and take at least six diamond tricks, and most likely seven.

Deal 21

1. Bid 2NT; break the transfer to show enthusiasm for clubs.

2. You hold ♣K-10-x. You also have 17 HCP and your points are made up mostly of aces and kings, but with that club holding you would break the transfer without all the rest!

3. Bid 4◇, a control-showing cuebid. Although you are not sure whether the final contract will be hearts or clubs, you can at least show your diamond ace, and then await developments. If partner bids 4♡ over your 4◇, you will pass.

Deal 22

1. You should simply accept the transfer and bid 3♣.

2. You do not have a top honor in clubs, and three clubs with two honors is not good enough. Add this fact to your 15 HCP and high cards consisting mostly of queens and jacks, and you definitely don't want to encourage partner.

Deal 23

1. Exception time! While it is true you do not have the ace or king of clubs, you do hold five to the queen-jack. That fifth club should compel you to break the transfer and bid 2NT.

2. If partner transferred you to diamonds instead, you would feel even better about breaking the transfer: your diamond support is excellent. You would bid 3♣ over 2NT .

Deal 24

1. No, do not transfer. Bid 3♠ immediately to show your sixth spade and game-forcing strength.

2. a) Over 3NT you will pass. This requires a lot of discipline but partner can have a lot of hands that just don't fit well.

   b) Over 4♣, bid 4◇ — a control-showing cuebid. Partner's 4♣ was a cuebid and showed interest in a spade contract.

   c) Over 4♡, bid 5◇. You would like to use Blackwood but you can't as you do not have a club control. If partner bids 5♠ over 5◇, you will pass: that bidding indicates that the partnership is missing the ace and king of clubs.

   d) Over 4♠ you will pass. By not bidding 4♣ or 4♡, partner is suggesting he does not hold the ♣ A or ♡A.

3. Partner cannot bid a new suit at the four-level unless he has a control, namely an ace. Since you are looking at both the ace and king of diamonds, you know partner is not.

Deal 25

1. Optimally you would like to play in clubs at the three-level, but do you think the opponents will allow that to happen?

2. Don't jump to 3♣, as that promises partner a game-forcing hand! You could transfer to clubs and then compete higher if the opponents get in the auction, but the best idea is to jam the bidding right up to the five-level immediately. By jumping to 5♣ you are telling partner there is no slam and you are preempting the opponents. Sure, you may go down one or two tricks but you become an awfully tough opponent when you prevent the opponents from finding their fit.

Deal 26

1. You are happy with just about anything partner does except transferring you to diamonds.

   a) Bid 2♡. With two four-card majors you show your hearts first after a Stayman bid.

   b) Bid 3♡. With four-card support and a maximum (four aces are worth more than 16), make a super-acceptance of hearts.

   c) Bid 3♠ for the same reason.

d) Bid 2NT. With ♣A-10-8, break the transfer.

e) Bid 3◇; a disciplined bid. You do not have a third diamond.

Deal 27

1. You should bid 3♣. Even though your hand looks beautiful, it is not so pretty in support of clubs. Make the disciplined bid of 3♣ and do not break the transfer.

2. Bid 3NT. Partner's 3♡ bid shows four hearts along with his six clubs. You don't have a fit with either of partner's two suits but you do have the other two suits well stopped.

Deal 28

1. Transfer to hearts. With 2 HCP, keep the contract low.

2. You should pass 3♡. While it is true partner may have the perfect hand with fitting honors in clubs and hearts, combined you still have at most 19 HCP, and most of the time 3♡ will be too high.

Deal 29

1. Do not bid 2NT! Remember that bid promises diamonds. You must begin with 2♣, Stayman, and then rebid 2NT to show a balanced hand with 8-9 HCP.

Deal 30

1. That six-card minor is so strong and that four-card major is so weak that it is tempting to jump to 3◇ immediately over 1NT. But you should begin by transferring to diamonds.

2. Partner surely will rebid 3◇. How can he possibly break the transfer when you are looking at solid diamonds?

3. You should rebid 3♠ to show your four-card major. You never know when partner is going to hold AKxx of spades.

Deal 31

1. You should break the transfer and bid 3♣. Remember when partner transfers you to a minor you will either bid that minor

or break the transfer by bidding in between. Don't even think about bidding 3♡ to show your five-card heart suit.

2. You should bid 3♣. With a third club you would break the transfer.
3. Bid 2♠. Only with a fourth spade should you consider super-accepting in spades.

Deal 32

1. Bid 2NT, transfer to diamonds.
2. If partner breaks the transfer with 3♣ you can bid 3NT with confidence. If partner bids 3♢, pass and play there. (If you visualize partner holding a small doubleton in diamonds, you can imagine how difficult it will be to make 3NT.)

Deal 33

1. Bid 3♣ next, natural and game forcing.
2. By rebidding 3♣ you create a game force and promise at least four good clubs. With two five-card suits and good controls, you could be in the slam range if partner fits one of your suits.
3. 3♠. After showing hearts and clubs this bid is an obvious control-showing cuebid. Partner will play you for first-round spade control.

Deal 34

1. 3NT.
2. You have 9 HCP and a six-card club suit. This hand is too strong to transfer to clubs, since you want to be in game. Will you be any better off when you hear partner does not like his hand for clubs? No. Therefore, as soon as partner opens 1NT you should plan to bid game.

Deal 35

1. You should bid 3♠. This bid shows a sixth spade and is invitational to game. Partner will pass or bid 4♠.
2. You would rebid 2♠, to play, in either case.

Deal 36

1. Although you could transfer to diamonds, bidding 4♣, Gerber, is best. If you do decide to transfer to diamonds, your next bid will be 4NT, RKB for diamonds. Warning: will you know what to do when partner shows two keycards?

2. After 4♣, Gerber:

   a) If partner shows one ace you will know the 'wheels fell off'. Looking at 15 HCP, you know it is impossible for partner to open the bidding with 1NT and have only one ace.

   b) Bid 5◇ (or 4NT), to play.

   c) Bid 6◇, to play.

   d) Bid 7NT. You can count thirteen tricks.

Deal 37

1. You should bid 2NT. Bidding 3♣ is a remote possibility, but that would show a game-forcing hand, and if partner has only 15 HCP he may not be happy with your bidding. With only 8 HCP you should just invite partner to game.

2. If partner bids 3♡ over your 2NT call, he is promising a third heart. Even though partner is prepared to stop in partscore, you can re-evaluate your hand for hearts and bid 4♡. You can count three support points for your singleton spade.

Deal 38

1. Imagine a hand in which partner has no heart honors: in 3NT the opponents might cash the first five heart tricks. Therefore, you should describe your hand's distribution and include partner in the decision-making process. Who knows, maybe a diamond game or slam is the best contract with the combined hands.

2. Partner will have at least three spades for his return to spades.

3. Bid 4♠. Although some slams might make when partner has a perfect hand and all the finesses are working, just 'take the money' with 4♠.

Deal 39

1. You plan to bid game if partner breaks the transfer; however you will settle for partscore if partner cannot do anything exciting.

2. You cannot be any more confident. This is the hand Four-suit Transfers are perfect for.

3. Oh, sure you would prefer to contribute a little more outside clubs than the jack of hearts, but you can't have everything. The only reason you are considering 3NT is that partner has K-x-x of clubs. The club king comprises three of his points and that will total six tricks. Surely with all his other HCP he should be able to muster up three additional tricks.

Deal 40

1. a) 2♡. After a 2♣ Stayman bid, always show hearts first when you hold two four-card majors.

   b) 3♡. By jumping to the three-level you show the super-accept which promises at least four hearts and a maximum strength hand.

   c) 3♠. Ditto but in this case you have four spades to go with partner's five or more.

   d) 2NT. Break the transfer to show your good hand for clubs.

   e) 3◇. Finally, a suit you can't super-accept as you are lacking a third diamond.

   f) 3◇. By bidding 3◇ you show club support and first-round diamond control.

   g) 3NT (or 4◇). You cannot bid any other suit as that would promise the ace in that suit.

   h) 4◇. Show the ace of diamonds and heart support.

   j) 4◇. Ditto but in this case you imply good spade support.

   k) Pass. We saved the easiest to the last!

Deal 1 - Dealer South

NORTH
♠ K 6
♡ K 5
◇ 8 5
♣ 10 8 7 6 4 3 2

SOUTH
♠ A 9 7 2
♡ Q J 10
◇ A Q 3
♣ K 9 5

NORTH	SOUTH
	1NT
2♠	2NT
3♣	pass

Deal 2 - Dealer South

NORTH
♠ —
♡ K Q 9 4
◇ 8 3
♣ A Q 8 7 6 4 3

SOUTH
♠ A Q 8
♡ J 8 3
◇ A K 4 2
♣ K 10 9

NORTH	SOUTH
	1NT
2♠	2NT
3♡	3♠
4♣	4◇
6♣	

Deal 3 - Dealer North

NORTH
♠ A K J 4
♡ K Q J 2
◇ 8 2
♣ Q 9 8

SOUTH
♠ 10 7 6
♡ 8 3
◇ K Q J 9 7 4
♣ 7 2

NORTH	SOUTH
1NT	2NT
3◇	pass

Deal 4 - Dealer North

NORTH
♠ A 10 3
♡ K 9 2
◇ A 10 8 4 2
♣ A 4

SOUTH
♠ Q J 8 4
♡ Q J
◇ Q J
♣ Q J 9 6 5

NORTH	SOUTH
1NT	2♣
2◇	3NT

Deal 5 - Dealer South

NORTH
♠ 7 4
♡ 9
◇ K Q 10 8 3
♣ A 9 7 5 3

SOUTH
♠ A 10 6 5
♡ A 7 3
◇ A 2
♣ K Q 8 4

NORTH	SOUTH
	1NT
2NT	3◇
4♣	4♡[1]
5♣	6♣

1. Cuebid, agreeing clubs.

Deal 6 - Dealer North

NORTH
♠ 9 7 5 3
♡ A K 4
◇ K Q 7 3
♣ A 4

SOUTH
♠ A 8
♡ 7
◇ A J 9 8 4
♣ K Q 10 7 2

NORTH	SOUTH
1NT	2NT
3♣[1]	4NT
5◇[2]	5♡[3]
5NT[4]	7◇

1. Super-accept.
2. Three keycards.
3. Queen-ask.
4. Trump queen and the ♡K.

Deal 7 - Dealer North

NORTH
♠ A Q 2
♡ Q J 4
◇ A 8 3
♣ K 10 9 8

SOUTH
♠ K 10 9 7 3
♡ A 3
◇ 4
♣ A J 7 6 5

NORTH	SOUTH
1NT	2♡
2♠	3♣
3◇[1]	3♡[2]
3♠[2]	4◇[2]
4NT	5♡[3]
6♣	

1. Cuebid, inferentially agreeing clubs as trumps.
2. Cuebid.
3. 2 keycards, no trump queen.

Deal 8 - Dealer South

NORTH
♠ A 5
♡ K 6
◇ A 8 4
♣ Q J 10 9 8 4

SOUTH
♠ K Q J 7
♡ Q J 9
◇ Q J 3 2
♣ K 7

NORTH	SOUTH
	1NT
3♣	3NT

Deal 9 - Dealer South

NORTH
♠ 7
♡ K 5 4
♢ K Q 9 7 6 4
♣ A 8 7

SOUTH
♠ Q 10 6 3
♡ A Q 10 9
♢ A J 8
♣ K 4

NORTH	SOUTH
	1NT
3♢	3♡¹
4♣²	4♢²
4♠²	6♢

1. Cuebid, inferentially agreeing diamonds as trumps.
2. Cuebid.

Deal 10 - Dealer North

NORTH
♠ A 3 2
♡ A 5 2
♢ A 4 3
♣ K 6 4 3

SOUTH
♠ J 9 8
♡ 10 6
♢ J 7
♣ 10 9 8 7 5 2

NORTH	SOUTH
1NT	2♠
2NT	3♣
pass	

Deal 11 - Dealer South

NORTH
♠ J
♡ J 6 3
♢ 7 6 4
♣ 10 7 6 5 4 3

SOUTH
♠ A 8 6
♡ K 9 7
♢ Q J 5
♣ A K 9 8

NORTH	SOUTH
	1NT
2♠	2NT
3♣	pass

Deal 12 - Dealer North

NORTH
♠ J 4 2
♡ A Q J 7
◇ Q 10
♣ K Q 9 5

☐

SOUTH
♠ K Q 6 3
♡ 8 3
◇ A J 9 7 6 4
♣ 7

NORTH	SOUTH
1NT	2NT
3◇	3♠
3NT	

Deal 13 - Dealer South

NORTH
♠ K J 10
♡ K 10 2
◇ A J 9 8
♣ K 7 2

☐

SOUTH
♠ Q 7
♡ Q 9 8
◇ K 4
♣ J 9 6 5 4 3

NORTH	SOUTH
	pass
1NT	2♣
2◇	2NT
pass	

Deal 14 - Dealer South

NORTH
♠ Q 10 7 6 4
♡ K J 8 7 2
◇ 3
♣ A 2

☐

SOUTH
♠ A K 5
♡ Q 10
◇ K Q J 9 4
♣ J 9 3

NORTH	SOUTH
	1NT
2♡	2♠
4♡	4♠

Deal 15 - Dealer North

NORTH
♠ A K 10 7
♡ 9 8 6
◇ K Q 2
♣ A J 8

□

SOUTH
♠ Q 8 6 5 3
♡ 4
◇ A 9 8 4 3
♣ 10 7

NORTH	SOUTH
1NT	2♡
3♠[1]	4♠

1. Super-accept of spades.

Deal 16 - Dealer South

NORTH
♠ K 9
♡ 8
◇ A 8 4 3
♣ K J 10 9 6 2

□

SOUTH
♠ A Q J
♡ K Q J 5
◇ Q J 5
♣ 8 7 4

NORTH	SOUTH
	1NT
2♠	3♣
3◇	3NT

Deal 17 - Dealer North

NORTH
♠ A Q 10
♡ K Q 10 9
◇ K J 5 4
♣ J 8

□

SOUTH
♠ 5 3 2
♡ 7 3
◇ 8 2
♣ A K Q 4 3 2

NORTH	SOUTH
1NT	3NT

Deal 18 - Dealer South

NORTH		NORTH	SOUTH
♠ 6			1NT
♡ K 8 5 4 2		2♠	3♣
◇ 9		3♡	3NT
♣ K Q 9 5 4 3		4♡	

SOUTH
♠ A Q 4
♡ Q J 9
◇ Q J 5 4 3
♣ A 8

Deal 19 - Dealer North

NORTH		NORTH	SOUTH
♠ A Q 10		1NT	2♠
♡ K Q 10 8		2NT	3NT
◇ J 10			
♣ A 9 7 4			

SOUTH
♠ 9 8
♡ 6
◇ Q 7 6 2
♣ K J 8 6 5 3

Deal 20 - Dealer South

NORTH		NORTH	SOUTH
♠ 10 2			1NT
♡ 9 4		2NT	3♣
◇ K 10 9 7 5 4 3		3NT	
♣ Q 8			

SOUTH
♠ K J 4 3
♡ A J 10
◇ A 8 2
♣ K J 7

Deal 21 - Dealer North

NORTH
♠ K 7 5 4
♡ K J 9 2
♢ A K
♣ K 10 8

[ ]

SOUTH
♠ Q 6
♡ A Q 8 7
♢ 7
♣ Q J 9 7 4 3

NORTH	SOUTH
1NT	2♠
2NT	3♡
4♢[1]	4♡

1. Cuebid.

Deal 22 - Dealer South

NORTH
♠ J 8 7
♡ 5 4
♢ 8 2
♣ K 10 9 7 6 5

[ ]

SOUTH
♠ Q J 3 2
♡ Q 9 8 3
♢ A K
♣ Q J 4

NORTH	SOUTH
	1NT
2♠	3♣
pass	

Deal 23 - Dealer North

NORTH
♠ A 4
♡ A 8 7
♢ A Q 9
♣ Q J 7 5 2

[ ]

SOUTH
♠ 10 9 3
♡ 6 4
♢ 8 2
♣ A K 9 8 6 4

NORTH	SOUTH
1NT	2♠
2NT	3NT

Deal 24 - Dealer South

NORTH
♠ A Q 10 8 6 5
♡ 8
♢ A K 3
♣ Q 7 3

☐

SOUTH
♠ K 7 4 3
♡ K J 2
♢ J 10
♣ A K 6 4

NORTH	SOUTH
	1NT
3♠	4♣[1]
4♢[1]	4♠
4NT	5♡[2]
6♠	

1. Cuebid.
2. Two keycards, no trump queen.

Deal 25 - Dealer North

NORTH
♠ A Q 10 8
♡ K J 4
♢ 10 7 3 2
♣ K Q

☐

SOUTH
♠ 6 4
♡ 5
♢ 4
♣ J 10 8 7 6 5 4 3 2

NORTH	SOUTH
1NT	5♣

Deal 26 - Dealer South

NORTH
♠ 6 4
♡ 8 5 3
♢ K 9
♣ K Q 9 7 5 3

☐

SOUTH
♠ A 10 7 3
♡ A 10 9 7
♢ A 10
♣ A 10 8

NORTH	SOUTH
	1NT
2♠	2NT
3NT	

Deal 27 - Dealer North

NORTH
♠ A Q 10
♡ K 10 9
◇ A K 10 9 8
♣ 9 8

SOUTH
♠ 4
♡ A J 8 3
◇ J 7
♣ A K 7 6 4 3

NORTH	SOUTH
1NT	2♠
3♣	3♡
3NT	

Deal 28 - Dealer South

NORTH
♠ 7
♡ J 9 7 5 4
◇ 6
♣ J 10 9 8 4 3

SOUTH
♠ K Q 5 4
♡ A Q 10 3
◇ K Q 7
♣ 7 6

NORTH	SOUTH
	1NT
2◇	3♡[1]
pass	

1. Super-accept of hearts.

Deal 29 - Dealer North

NORTH
♠ Q 2
♡ K J 10 3
◇ A Q 4
♣ K 9 4 3

SOUTH
♠ A J 4
♡ 9 8 6
◇ K 10 8 3
♣ J 7 2

NORTH	SOUTH
1NT	2♣
2♡	2NT
pass	

Deal 30 - Dealer South

NORTH
♠ 8 6 4 3
♡ 9
◇ A K Q J 7 6
♣ A 3

☐

SOUTH
♠ A K 9 2
♡ K Q J
◇ 9 2
♣ K 9 8 2

NORTH	SOUTH
	1NT
2NT	3◇
3♠	4♠

Deal 31 - Dealer North

NORTH
♠ A 6 3
♡ K Q J 9 6
◇ K 10 3
♣ K 3

☐

SOUTH
♠ J 10 9
♡ 10
◇ A Q 9 8 6 4
♣ 9 6 5

NORTH	SOUTH
1NT	2NT
3♣	3NT

Deal 32 - Dealer South

NORTH
♠ 9 7
♡ 6 4 3
◇ A J 10 9 7 5
♣ Q 5

☐

SOUTH
♠ A J 3
♡ K Q J
◇ 3 2
♣ A J 7 4 2

NORTH	SOUTH
	1NT
2NT	3◇
pass	

Deal 33 - Dealer North

NORTH
♠ K 10 9 5
♡ Q 3
◇ A K 5
♣ K Q 10 5

SOUTH
♠ A 7
♡ K 10 8 7 6
◇ 2
♣ A 9 7 6 4

NORTH	SOUTH
1NT	2◇
2♡	3♣
3◇[1]	3♠[2]
4◇[2]	4NT
5♠[3]	6♣

1. Cuebid, inferentially agreeing clubs as trumps.
2. Cuebid.
3. Two keycards with the ♣Q.

Deal 34 - Dealer South

NORTH
♠ K 5
♡ J 10 4
◇ J 9
♣ A 10 9 8 4 3

SOUTH
♠ A J 7 3
♡ K 9 8 5
◇ K Q 7
♣ K 7

NORTH	SOUTH
	1NT
3NT	

Deal 35 - Dealer North

NORTH
♠ J 4
♡ Q J 9 4
◇ K J 10
♣ A K 3 2

SOUTH
♠ K Q 8 7 6 5
♡ 10 8 3
◇ 7 3
♣ Q 4

NORTH	SOUTH
1NT	2♡
2♠	3♠
pass	

Deal 36 - Dealer South

NORTH
♠ K 3
♡ K 5
◇ K Q J 10 8 6 4
♣ K 2

☐

SOUTH
♠ A J 8 4
♡ A Q 9 8
◇ 7 2
♣ A 10 3

NORTH	SOUTH
	1NT
4♣	4NT[1]
6◇	

1. Three aces.

Deal 37 - Dealer North

NORTH
♠ K Q J 4
♡ Q 5 4
◇ A J 3 2
♣ Q 9

☐

SOUTH
♠ 7
♡ A 10 9 7 3
◇ 9 7 6
♣ K J 4 3

NORTH	SOUTH
1NT	2◇
2♡	2NT
3♡	pass

Deal 38 - Dealer South

NORTH
♠ K 10 9 4 3
♡ 3
◇ Q J 7 6
♣ A 8 6

☐

SOUTH
♠ A J 7
♡ A Q 2
◇ K 9 5
♣ Q 10 3 2

NORTH	SOUTH
	1NT
2♡	2♠
3◇	3♠
4♠	

Deal 39 - Dealer North

NORTH
♠ Q J 9 5
♡ K Q 10
◇ A J 10
♣ K 6 5

□

SOUTH
♠ 10 8
♡ J 3 2
◇ 5 4
♣ A Q 10 8 7 4

NORTH	SOUTH
1NT	2♠
2NT	3NT

Deal 40 - Dealer South

NORTH
♠ A 9
♡ K 8
◇ Q J 8 7 6 5
♣ Q 8 4

□

SOUTH
♠ K J 8 3
♡ Q 10 9 4
◇ A K
♣ K J 9

NORTH	SOUTH
	1NT
3NT[1]	

1. The chances that partner has super diamonds and all the other exact cards you will need for slam are just too remote.

section
PRACTICE HANDS 6

Hand 1 - Dealer South

♠ K 6
♡ K 5
◇ 8 5
♣ 10 8 7 6 4 3 2

YOUR AUCTION

NORTH	SOUTH

Hand 2 - Dealer South

♠ —
♡ K Q 9 4
◇ 8 3
♣ A Q 8 7 6 4 3

YOUR AUCTION

NORTH	SOUTH

Hand 3 - Dealer North

♠ A K J 4
♡ K Q J 2
◇ 8 2
♣ Q 9 8

YOUR AUCTION

NORTH	SOUTH

Hand 4 - Dealer North

♠ A 10 3
♡ K 9 2
◇ A 10 8 4 2
♣ A 4

YOUR AUCTION

NORTH	SOUTH

Hand 5 - Dealer South

♠ 7 4
♡ 9
◇ K Q 10 8 3
♣ A 9 7 5 3

YOUR AUCTION

NORTH	SOUTH

Hand 6 - Dealer North

♠ 9 7 5 3
♡ A K 4
◇ K Q 7 3
♣ A 4

YOUR AUCTION

NORTH	SOUTH

Hand 7 - Dealer North

♠ A Q 2
♡ Q J 4
◇ A 8 3
♣ K 10 9 8

YOUR AUCTION

NORTH	SOUTH

Hand 8 - Dealer South

♠ A 5
♡ K 6
◇ A 8 4
♣ Q J 10 9 8 4

YOUR AUCTION

NORTH	SOUTH

Hand 9 - Dealer South

♠ 7
♡ K 5 4
◇ K Q 9 7 6 4
♣ A 8 7

YOUR AUCTION

NORTH	SOUTH

Hand 10 - Dealer North

♠ A 3 2
♡ A 5 2
◇ A 4 3
♣ K 6 4 3

YOUR AUCTION

NORTH	SOUTH

Hand 11 - Dealer South

♠ J
♡ J 6 3
♢ 7 6 4
♣ 10 7 6 5 4 3

YOUR AUCTION

NORTH	SOUTH

Hand 12 - Dealer North

♠ J 4 2
♡ A Q J 7
♢ Q 10
♣ K Q 9 5

YOUR AUCTION

NORTH	SOUTH

Hand 13 - Dealer South

♠ K J 10
♡ K 10 2
♢ A J 9 8
♣ K 7 2

YOUR AUCTION

NORTH	SOUTH

Hand 14 - Dealer South

♠ Q 10 7 6 4
♡ K J 8 7 2
♢ 3
♣ A 2

YOUR AUCTION

NORTH	SOUTH

Hand 15 - Dealer North

♠ A K 10 7
♡ 9 8 6
♢ K Q 2
♣ A J 8

YOUR AUCTION

NORTH	SOUTH

Hand 16 - Dealer South

♠ K 9
♡ 8
◇ A 8 4 3
♣ K J 10 9 6 2

YOUR AUCTION

NORTH	SOUTH

Hand 17 - Dealer North

♠ A Q 10
♡ K Q 10 9
◇ K J 5 4
♣ J 8

YOUR AUCTION

NORTH	SOUTH

Hand 18 - Dealer South

♠ 6
♡ K 8 5 4 2
◇ 9
♣ K Q 9 5 4 3

YOUR AUCTION

NORTH	SOUTH

Hand 19 - Dealer North

♠ A Q 10
♡ K Q 10 8
◇ J 10
♣ A 9 7 4

YOUR AUCTION

NORTH	SOUTH

Hand 20 - Dealer South

♠ 10 2
♡ 9 4
◇ K 10 9 7 5 4 3
♣ Q 8

YOUR AUCTION

NORTH	SOUTH

Hand 21 - Dealer North

♠ K 7 5 4
♡ K J 9 2
♢ A K
♣ K 10 8

YOUR AUCTION

NORTH   SOUTH

Hand 22 - Dealer South

♠ J 8 7
♡ 5 4
♢ 8 2
♣ K 10 9 7 6 5

YOUR AUCTION

NORTH   SOUTH

Hand 23 - Dealer North

♠ A 4
♡ A 8 7
♢ A Q 9
♣ Q J 7 5 2

YOUR AUCTION

NORTH   SOUTH

Hand 24 - Dealer South

♠ A Q 10 8 6 5
♡ 8
♢ A K 3
♣ Q 7 3

YOUR AUCTION

NORTH   SOUTH

Hand 25 - Dealer North

♠ A Q 10 8
♡ K J 4
♢ 10 7 3 2
♣ K Q

YOUR AUCTION

NORTH   SOUTH

Hand 26 - Dealer South

♠ 6 4
♡ 8 5 3
◇ K 9
♣ K Q 9 7 5 3

YOUR AUCTION

NORTH	SOUTH

Hand 27 - Dealer North

♠ A Q 10
♡ K 10 9
◇ A K 10 9 8
♣ 9 8

YOUR AUCTION

NORTH	SOUTH

Hand 28 - Dealer South

♠ 7
♡ J 9 7 5 4
◇ 6
♣ J 10 9 8 4 3

YOUR AUCTION

NORTH	SOUTH

Hand 29 - Dealer North

♠ Q 2
♡ K J 10 3
◇ A Q 3
♣ K 9 4 2

YOUR AUCTION

NORTH	SOUTH

Hand 30 - Dealer South

♠ 8 6 4 3
♡ 9
◇ A K Q J 7 6
♣ A 3

YOUR AUCTION

NORTH	SOUTH

Hand 31 - Dealer North

♠ A 6 3
♡ K Q J 9 6
◇ K 10 3
♣ K 3

YOUR AUCTION

NORTH	SOUTH

Hand 32 - Dealer South

♠ 9 7
♡ 6 4 3
◇ A J 10 9 7 5
♣ Q 5

YOUR AUCTION

NORTH	SOUTH

Hand 33 - Dealer North

♠ K 10 9 5
♡ Q 3
◇ A K 5
♣ K Q 10 5

YOUR AUCTION

NORTH	SOUTH

Hand 34 - Dealer South

♠ K 5
♡ J 10 4
◇ J 9
♣ A 10 9 8 4 3

YOUR AUCTION

NORTH	SOUTH

Hand 35 - Dealer North

♠ J 4
♡ Q J 9 4
◇ K J 10
♣ A K 3 2

YOUR AUCTION

NORTH	SOUTH

Hand 36 - Dealer South

♠ K 3
♡ K 5
◇ K Q J 10 8 6 4
♣ K 2

YOUR AUCTION

NORTH	SOUTH

Hand 37 - Dealer North

♠ K Q J 4
♡ Q 5 4
◇ A J 3 2
♣ Q 9

YOUR AUCTION

NORTH	SOUTH

Hand 38 - Dealer South

♠ K 10 9 4 3
♡ 3
◇ Q J 7 6
♣ A 8 6

YOUR AUCTION

NORTH	SOUTH

Hand 39 - Dealer South

♠ Q J 9 5
♡ K Q 10
◇ A J 10
♣ K 6 5

YOUR AUCTION

NORTH	SOUTH

Hand 40 - Dealer North

♠ A 9
♡ K 8
◇ Q J 8 7 6 5
♣ Q 8 4

YOUR AUCTION

NORTH	SOUTH

Hand 1 - Dealer South

♠ A 9 7 2
♡ Q J 10
◇ A Q 3
♣ K 9 5

YOUR AUCTION

NORTH   SOUTH

Hand 2 - Dealer South

♠ A Q 8
♡ J 8 3
◇ A K 4 2
♣ K 10 9

YOUR AUCTION

NORTH   SOUTH

Hand 3 - Dealer North

♠ 10 7 6
♡ 8 3
◇ K Q J 9 7 4
♣ 7 2

YOUR AUCTION

NORTH   SOUTH

Hand 4 - Dealer North

♠ Q J 8 4
♡ Q J
◇ Q J
♣ Q J 9 6 5

YOUR AUCTION

NORTH   SOUTH

Hand 5 - Dealer South

♠ A 10 6 5
♡ A 7 3
◇ A 2
♣ K Q 8 4

YOUR AUCTION

NORTH   SOUTH

Hand 6 - Dealer North

♠ A 8
♡ 7
◇ A J 9 8 4
♣ K Q 10 7 2

YOUR AUCTION

NORTH	SOUTH

Hand 7 - Dealer North

♠ K 10 9 7 3
♡ A 3
◇ 4
♣ A J 7 6 5

YOUR AUCTION

NORTH	SOUTH

Hand 8 - Dealer South

♠ K Q J 7
♡ Q J 9
◇ Q J 3 2
♣ K 7

YOUR AUCTION

NORTH	SOUTH

Hand 9 - Dealer South

♠ Q 10 6 3
♡ A Q 10 9
◇ A J 8
♣ K 4

YOUR AUCTION

NORTH	SOUTH

Hand 10 - Dealer North

♠ J 9 8
♡ 10 6
◇ J 7
♣ 10 9 8 7 5 2

YOUR AUCTION

NORTH	SOUTH

Hand 11 - Dealer South

♠ A 8 6
♡ K 9 7
◇ Q J 5
♣ A K 9 8

YOUR AUCTION

NORTH	SOUTH

Hand 12 - Dealer North

♠ K Q 6 3
♡ 8 3
◇ A J 9 7 6 4
♣ 7

YOUR AUCTION

NORTH	SOUTH

Hand 13 - Dealer South

♠ Q 7
♡ Q 9 8
◇ K 4
♣ J 9 6 5 4 3

YOUR AUCTION

NORTH	SOUTH

Hand 14 - Dealer South

♠ A K 5
♡ Q 10
◇ K Q J 9 4
♣ J 9 3

YOUR AUCTION

NORTH	SOUTH

Hand 15 - Dealer North

♠ Q 8 6 5 3
♡ 4
◇ A 9 8 4 3
♣ 10 7

YOUR AUCTION

NORTH	SOUTH

Hand 16 - Dealer South

♠ A Q J
♡ K Q J 5
◇ Q J 5
♣ 8 7 4

YOUR AUCTION

NORTH	SOUTH

Hand 17 - Dealer North

♠ 5 3 2
♡ 7 3
◇ 8 2
♣ A K Q 4 3 2

YOUR AUCTION

NORTH	SOUTH

Hand 18 - Dealer South

♠ A Q 4
♡ Q J 9
◇ Q J 5 4 3
♣ A 8

YOUR AUCTION

NORTH	SOUTH

Hand 19 - Dealer North

♠ 9 8
♡ 6
◇ Q 7 6 2
♣ K J 8 6 5 3

YOUR AUCTION

NORTH	SOUTH

Hand 20 - Dealer South

♠ K J 4 3
♡ A J 10
◇ A 8 2
♣ K J 7

YOUR AUCTION

NORTH	SOUTH

Hand 21 - Dealer North

♠ Q 6
♡ A Q 8 7
◇ 7
♣ Q J 9 7 4 3

YOUR AUCTION

NORTH	SOUTH

Hand 22 - Dealer South

♠ Q J 3 2
♡ Q 9 8 3
◇ A K
♣ Q J 4

YOUR AUCTION

NORTH	SOUTH

Hand 23 - Dealer North

♠ 10 9 3
♡ 6 4
◇ 8 2
♣ A K 9 8 6 4

YOUR AUCTION

NORTH	SOUTH

Hand 24 - Dealer South

♠ K 7 5 3
♡ K J 2
◇ J 10
♣ A K 6 4

YOUR AUCTION

NORTH	SOUTH

Hand 25 - Dealer North

♠ 6 4
♡ 5
◇ 4
♣ J 10 8 7 6 5 4 3 2

YOUR AUCTION

NORTH	SOUTH

Hand 26 - Dealer South

♠ A 10 7 3
♡ A 10 9 7
◇ A 10
♣ A 10 8

YOUR AUCTION

NORTH	SOUTH

Hand 27 - Dealer North

♠ 4
♡ A J 8 3
◇ J 7
♣ A K 7 6 4 3

YOUR AUCTION

NORTH	SOUTH

Hand 28 - Dealer South

♠ K Q 5 4
♡ A Q 10 3
◇ K Q 7
♣ 7 6

YOUR AUCTION

NORTH	SOUTH

Hand 29 - Dealer North

♠ A J 4
♡ 9 8 6
◇ K 10 8 3
♣ J 7 2

YOUR AUCTION

NORTH	SOUTH

Hand 30 - Dealer South

♠ A K 9 2
♡ K Q J
◇ 9 2
♣ K 9 8 2

YOUR AUCTION

NORTH	SOUTH

Hand 31 - Dealer North

♠ J 10 9
♡ 10
◇ A Q 9 8 6 4
♣ 9 6 5

YOUR AUCTION

NORTH	SOUTH

Hand 32 - Dealer South

♠ A J 3
♡ K Q J
◇ 3 2
♣ A J 7 4 2

YOUR AUCTION

NORTH	SOUTH

Hand 33 - Dealer North

♠ A 7
♡ K 10 8 7 6
◇ 2
♣ A 9 7 6 4

YOUR AUCTION

NORTH	SOUTH

Hand 34 - Dealer South

♠ A J 7 3
♡ K 9 8 5
◇ K Q 7
♣ K 7

YOUR AUCTION

NORTH	SOUTH

Hand 35 - Dealer North

♠ K Q 8 7 6 5
♡ 10 8 3
◇ 7 3
♣ Q 4

YOUR AUCTION

NORTH	SOUTH

Hand 36 - Dealer South

♠ A J 8 4
♡ A Q 9 8
◇ 7 2
♣ A 10 3

YOUR AUCTION

NORTH	SOUTH

Hand 37 - Dealer North

♠ 7
♡ A J 9 7 3
◇ 9 7 6
♣ K J 4 3

YOUR AUCTION

NORTH	SOUTH

Hand 38 - Dealer South

♠ A J 7
♡ A Q 2
◇ K 9 5
♣ Q 10 3 2

YOUR AUCTION

NORTH	SOUTH

Hand 39 - Dealer North

♠ 10 8
♡ J 3 2
◇ 5 4
♣ A Q 10 8 7 4

YOUR AUCTION

NORTH	SOUTH

Hand 40 - Dealer South

♠ K J 8 3
♡ Q 10 9 4
◇ A K
♣ K J 9

YOUR AUCTION

NORTH	SOUTH